Mind Play for Match Play

Outsmarting your brain and your opponent in head to head golf

Tracy Tresidder

Copyright ©Tracy Tresidder 2012

Mind Play for Match Play: Outsmarting your brain and your opponent in head to head golf

Published January 2012

Acorn Press
Unit 8, 16-18 Clearview Place
Brookvale NSW 2100
Australia

Other books by same author:
Golf Mind Play: Outsmarting your brain to play your BEST golf
Published 2007, 2009

The National Library of Australia Cataloguing-in-Publication entry:

Tresidder, Tracy, 1958- .

Mind Play for Match Play: Outsmarting your brain and your opponent in head to head golf

1st ed.

ISBN 97809804282-2-3

1. Golf - Psychological aspects. 2. Golf - Coaching.

3. Golf.

I. Title.

796.352019

Golf Mind Play
www.golfmindplay.com
tracy@golfmindplay.com
+61 2 9924 7078
+61 415 980 476

Dedication

*To all who love the game as much
as I do.*

Tracy Tresidder

*"Your future will look like your present
until you practise something new to make it
different."*

Brian Cooke, inspirational leadership coach

Acknowledgements

There are many people I need to thank for helping with the creation of this book. Firstly my playing partners and fellow Pennant team members who have been an inspiration to be with as we share the delights and challenges of Match Play.

The eye for detail of my two wonderfully insightful editors, Janie Gilmour and Daniel Mitchell, has been very much appreciated.

I'm pleased to include observations from Jacqui Morgan and Tony McAllister Jnr, both top golfers at their respective clubs, whom I interviewed extensively for this book. Also thanks to my friends and fellow golfers, especially Sue and Gill, who have reviewed and commented on the manuscript.

To some of the greatest golf mind coaches on the planet - Harvey Penick, Dr Bob Rotella and Dr Joseph Parent - their wise words and expertise continue to guide me in all my work.

And last but not least to my gorgeous family – my husband Mike and sons Adam and Ben, who have not complained when things have fallen by the wayside when I have been too occupied with writing. I am indebted to them for their love and patience.

Contents

INTRODUCTION

Match play is golf's ultimate mind game.

Pitting golfer against golfer in a format where raw scores are irrelevant, match play is inherently different from stroke play, so it calls for a different mentality.

In stroke play, where scores are tallied for each hole and totalled at the end of the game, the golfer's primary concern is the course itself. Match play, on the other hand, requires keeping a watchful eye on the opposition, without paying them too much attention. Reading their mood. Deciphering their strengths and weaknesses. Adjusting tactics based on score and momentum.

Birdies, pars and bogeys? In match play they're meaningless. All that matters is beating your foe's result on each hole. You can make a triple-bogey (or worse) and still win a hole. You can make a birdie and lose one. You may even post a higher score than your foe for the entire round, yet emerge victorious.

That's part of what makes match play so compelling.

Watch the Presidents Cup, the Ryder Cup, or the Women's World Match Play and you'll understand. The head-to-head element fundamentally changes how players approach each shot. Because the tides can shift at any time, match play tends to favour golfers who perform well under pressure, and rewards those who maintain an awareness of their opponent's game as well as their own.

Match play presents endless mental challenges. Success often rides on one's ability to cope with the stress of a big deficit, or fending off overconfidence when comfortably ahead. Some golfers thrive when backed against a wall, while others are at ease when playing from out front. Few are equally good at both.

The hole-by-hole, all-or-nothing nature of match play encourages risk-taking and fierce competition, testing the limits of golfers at any skill level, both physically and mentally. That's why many competitive types prefer match play to stroke play - matches provide a forum for directly engaging an opponent and upping the psychological ante.

This book – the follow-up to *Golf Mind Play: Outsmarting your brain to play your BEST golf* – offers a comprehensive guide to excelling at match play. In it, I cover everything from match play's basic format and rules, to preparing yourself for a match, winning match play strategies, maximising opportunities that are presented and, of course, succeeding with a sound mental approach.

While the book's content is appropriate for anyone who competes in match play, including club championship and knockout events, it is particularly aimed at current and potential participants in the widely popular Pennant competition. Here golfers are given the opportunity to play as part of a group, pitting club teams against one another, with winners advancing to regional and state competition. Male and female amateurs of all handicap levels take part in these fun and often highly competitive events.

Whatever form of match play you'll be playing, I'm sure you will find plenty of helpful advice in the following pages.

I

THE BASICS OF MATCH PLAY

"You may know how to strike the ball BUT you need to learn how to play the game."

Sean Lynch, top golf mental coach

Match play is the purest form of golf competition — one golfer (or team) is pitted against another in a hole-to-hole challenge. For match play, golfers need a clear mind and sound preparation to manage the head-to-head confrontation and balancing act of a game that's very different from stroke play.

In this chapter, you'll learn the fundamentals of match play along with a few key points.

How it is Played

Match play follows a very simple scoring method as described in the Rules of Golf, set forth by the game's governing bodies, the R&A and United States Golf Association (USGA).

Essentially, the player or team with the fewest strokes on a hole wins the hole. If both sides make the same score, the hole is 'halved' or tied. The player/team winning the most holes wins the match.

It's possible (even common) to win a match without playing an entire 18 holes. This happens when one side leads by more holes than remain in the round. For example, if Player A leads by 3 after 16 holes, the match is won.

Rules & Etiquette

Before you enter a match play competition, it's important to be very clear on the rules and etiquette that deviate from stroke play convention. In many cases, what's considered a mere breach of etiquette in stroke play can result in actual consequences in match play.

A good example regards the rules for playing order. Once it's established who has the honour (i.e. plays first) on the opening hole, the honour is then determined by who won the previous hole; if that hole was halved, then it would be the winner of the hole before that one.

While playing out of turn may be deemed poor form in stroke play, in match play your opponent can legally request that you replay the shot — and you can rest assured that if your effort was long and straight, you'll be hitting from the same spot again!

A classic example here is putting out. Let's say you have the honour with a long putt, and your attempt places you a few centimetres from the hole. Out of habit you walk up to the ball and tap it in. As your opponent was still to play and their ball was farther from the hole, it was actually their turn to play so they can ask you to replace the ball and replay it. This now puts enormous pressure on you to sink the putt, and believe me when I say I have seen many a golfer miss putts from just a few centimetres! So always check who has the honour before hitting.

Of course, not all match play rules are pitted against the offender. Let's say your ball hits an opponent. In stroke play that's considered 'rub of the green', meaning you accept the result and play on, whereas match play rules give you the option to replay the shot without penalty. Similarly, there is no penalty for your ball hitting another player's ball on the green.

If your opponent plays out of turn you may ask them to play again. However, beware! Consider the possible consequences. They may hit a better shot the second time. They may become more determined and ramp up their game. But most importantly, your own game can be affected if deep down you have created an awkward situation that you are not comfortable with.

The general penalty for a match play infraction is usually **loss of hole**, but can be a maximum of two holes for violations such as too many clubs in your bag. A serious breach of the rules may even lead to disqualification, for example when a player deliberately breaks the rules. Don't dwell on this too much. Grab your rule book, which should always be in your bag, and stick some post-it notes on key items to help as a quick reference. A good start is Rule 2 Match Play and Rule 30 Three-Ball, Best Ball and Four-Ball Match Play.

The complete rules for match play are available through the R&A (www.randa.org), Golf Australia (www.golfaustralia.org.au) and USGA (www.usga.org) websites. These include any new changes to the Rules of Golf.

Singles & Team Play

Match play can be contested in singles (one-on-one) or in foursomes (two-on-two), also called 'fourball'. In singles, the two players compete for each hole. In fourball, each team submits the lowest score of its two players for each hole. So, if the two players on Team A make a 5 and a 4, the 4 is submitted against the other team's best score.

A third, less common format is called 'foursomes' or 'alternate shot'. Each team plays only one ball, with teammates alternating shots until the ball is holed. For example, Player A drives, Player B hits the approach shot, Player A attempts the first putt, and so forth.

Handicap Allowance

When using handicaps in individual match play, the lower handicap is subtracted from the higher one to determine how many strokes the higher handicap player receives. For example, if Player A holds a 10 handicap to Player B's 15, Player B receives five strokes (one each on the course's top five match index handicap holes, found on the back of the scorecard). Player A receives no strokes.

To elaborate, Player B's gross score on each of these five match index holes is reduced by one stroke. Therefore, a 5 becomes a net 4 and is matched against Player A's score to determine the winner.

Fourball handicap match play incorporates players' individual handicaps in a similar manner. The player with the smallest handicap is lowered to a scratch (or '0'), while the other players' handicaps are determined by subtracting the scratch player's initial handicap.

Example: If Player A is a 6 handicap and the other three all have handicaps of 16, the player with a 6 would be considered a scratch while the others would each play to a 10, receiving strokes on the top 10 match index handicap holes.

Things differ in Scratch or Pennant competitions where handicaps are left out of the equation, so neither player receives strokes and only gross scores are counted. However, if you are playing in a Pennants team for your club, it's important that you know your exact handicap before the team commences play because if anyone plays out of handicap order, that player or possibly the entire team may be disqualified.

Scoring & Terminology

Match play encompasses its own terminology, as distinct from stroke play. During a match play game, you will inevitably hear terms such as 'all square', 'dormie', '1-up', 'halved', '4 and 3' and so on. At first the jargon might be confusing, but the definitions will become second nature once you understand how the scoring works.

• 'All Square'

At the beginning of the match, competitors are labelled 'all square' or tied (starting at zero). The player who first wins a hole is said to be '1-up' or leading by one hole. If the leader wins the next two holes, he is '3-up' while the opponent who is trailing by three holes would be '3-down'. At any point when both players have won an equal number of holes, the match is 'all square' or tied.

When both players submit the same score on a hole, the hole is 'halved', squared or tied. Ties in match play do not count and are not recorded, as no hole has been awarded to either side.

• *Taking the Match 'Dormie'*

There comes a point in most games where the match goes 'dormie', meaning the leader is ahead by as many holes as there are remaining to finish 18. From this point, the trailing player must win every hole to tie the game. When a player takes a match dormie, they can no longer lose — they will either win or tie.

If the leader has taken the match dormie and wins or halves the next hole, the match is over regardless of how many of the 18 holes remain. For instance, if the players have just finished hole 15 and the leader is 3-up, then wins or halves the 16th hole, the remaining two holes are not played.

This of course is reliant on it being an 18-hole match play competition. If the match is to be played until there is a clear winner then it may continue for a few more holes.

• *Final Scores*

The final score of a match indicates whether the match ended early, or if it was taken to the 18th hole. A final score of 1-up means the contenders played through the entire 18 holes. A final score of 2-up indicates a player took the match dormie on the 17th hole and clinched the victory by winning the 18th.

A final score of 2 and 1 indicates the leader was ahead by two holes, with one hole remaining. The same applies to final scores 3 and 2 (3 holes up with 2 remaining), 4 and 3, and so forth. In short, the first number is the size of the lead, and the second number indicates the number of holes left unplayed when victory was secured.

Making Concessions

Conceded putts, although illegal in stroke play, are allowed in match play. If a player has a short putt to make, their opponent may declare the putt 'good' or 'it's your hole', as with a 'gimme' during an informal round. Keep in mind that this 'gimme' still counts as a shot.

A player may concede a stroke at any point on a hole, so the unplayed stroke is considered to be holed. For instance, if Player A has put two balls in the water and their opponent is on the green in two strokes, Player A may decide to concede so as to avoid wasting mental and physical energy on a hole that is already lost. Player B wins the hole with a score of 3.

Concessions are not mandatory, no matter how short the remaining putt nor how far behind a player has fallen on a hole. Players cannot ask an opponent for a concession, so never assume that you will get one, even if your ball is teetering on the edge of the cup. Always clarify with your opponent before you pick up your ball.

It's important to remember that a concession cannot be withdrawn after it has been made, so it's wise to decide beforehand how you'll deal with concessions early in the game.

Concession protocol as a strategic tactic is discussed in Chapter III.

Tips

1. Be well prepared by knowing how the match play rules differ from stroke play — you may be surprised how often a rules question comes up while playing a match.

2. Even though it is not required to keep a score, it is a good idea to write down the number of strokes each player took to hole out – just in case there are any discrepancies or disputes.

3. Consider conceding short putts early and often. This prevents your opponent from having the chance to putt from these distances and later in the match, when the pressure is on and you ask them to putt out their nervousness may cause them to miss this easy putt.

II

PREPARING FOR THE MATCH

"Without goals, and plans to reach them, you are like a ship that has set sail with no destination."

Fitzhugh Dodson, noted psychologist and educator

A successful player, either in team and individual match play, always goes to the tee well prepared. They've practised the right way, studied the course and conditioned their mind to focus on the process of hitting shots, not on the results.

Team match play competition presents a unique challenge — finding a partner with whom you have chemistry. It's important to get along, of course, but the ideal partner will complement both your game and personality.

This chapter will help you get the most from your pre-match prep work.

Choosing a Partner

In a fourball match, it's wise to pick a partner who complements your playing style and vice versa. This could mean pairing a player with a strong short game with one whose long game is solid, or matching an aggressive golfer with a conservative one. Choosing a partner with opposing skills and demeanour will allow you to find solutions in difficult situations — at the very least it will offer more strategic options.

In foursomes, where team mates alternate hitting shots with the same ball, it's advantageous to play with someone who shares your style, hits similar distances and plays the same way. Why? Because it's easier to play from positions where both of you would normally drive the ball, rather than from unfamiliar spots on (or off) the fairway. This is especially true when playing your home course, where you're accustomed to hitting approaches from a certain distance on each hole.

Above all, choosing a partner you're comfortable with is paramount. Both foursomes and fourball require partners to make many joint decisions, so any underlying tensions can disrupt a team's performance quickly. Golfers with complementary personalities are better able to maintain strong morale throughout 18 holes.

Using a Caddie

Depending on the conditions of play for your competition, you may be allowed to have a caddie. Choose someone who knows your golf well, who can give you good advice and who knows when you're in need of food or drink. Before the match, show them which clubs you prefer to use in particular situations and run over your general game plan with them.

However, during the match, don't chat with them – save that for afterwards. They should be an asset to your game.

Having a caddie may also assist you from a gamesmanship perspective. For example, if you find your opponent is a chatty character but you would prefer to concentrate with little conversation, a good tactic is to ask your caddie to always stand between you and your opponent. This way your opponent can annoy your caddie, not you.

Another tactic is for your caddie to be very friendly to your opponent - this may well cause your opponent to relax and their concentration to lapse. Keep in mind that whatever tactic you choose to employ must not affect your game, so if you are uncomfortable with it, don't do it.

When you've made it to the finals you'll probably find you have a referee for your match. Don't be daunted by this - use it to your favour. The referee will relieve you of any stress you may feel about the rules. Their job is to monitor the match, pick up any rule infringements and be there for advice if you're unsure about anything.

Before the match the referee will note which balls you and your opponent are using and they'll also advise you of any Local Rules and rules for the game.

Practice Routine

In the days leading up to a match, your practice sessions should be geared toward preparing for the course itself, while fine-tuning your short game. It's imperative to spend time at the driving range, and also in the practice bunker and on the putting green, to ensure you are fully prepared.

Some courses allow you to play a practice round the week or two before your match. Take advantage of this opportunity, as this will help develop your confidence, as you'll be more familiar with the layout. (See 'Know the Course' later in this chapter for tips on gathering information.) According to match play rules you are also allowed onto the course on the day of your competition, so use this chance to practise chipping and putting around the ninth or 18th greens.

The course's characteristics should dictate portions of your practice. Let's say you're competing over a course with tight fairways. Spend a little extra time working on your driving accuracy and alignment. If windy conditions are forecast, practice the punch shot or bump-and-run technique.

Solid putting, chipping and pitching will always serve you well in match play. In fact, nothing is more frustrating than a foe who continually saves par from off the green, or holes out routinely from 2 metres or more. Thorough short game practice will also give you a good feel for the club come match day.

"A week before the match is all about your hands," notes Tony McAllister, a single-figure marker with years of match play experience.

The method known as 'random practice' is a great way to prepare in the run-up to an event. Rather than hitting multiple shots with one club, then moving to the next club and proceeding through the bag, emulate your on-course play on the range. For instance, start by hitting a single shot with the driver, followed by a 6-iron, then a wedge. Vary your shot shapes and swing length, as you do when faced with different conditions in an actual round. And always aim for a specific target, such as a flag or distant tree.

If you're playing in a fourball with a partner, then get out there and practice with them, ideally on the course where the match will be held. No matter how well you know each other, don't wait until an hour before the match to discuss tactics.

If you're playing in a Pennant team, get together with your club's pro for a lesson or two, then organize a practice session with the rest of the team using the 'random practice' method, just mentioned.

If you are a higher handicapper and always play with other high handicappers, part of your preparation leading up to an event should include playing with others with much lower handicaps. The first thing you will notice is that they don't hit the ball much better than you do. However, you should observe how they can save themselves after a shot into the trees with a well thought out next shot that will have them complete the hole with a bogey, not a double or a disaster.

Also consider things like club selection — avoiding that bunker you go into every other game. Watch them put that driver away and hit 3-wood, 3-wood, wedge to that long par 4. Learn from their course management strategy, taking note of the decisions they make when faced with more difficult shots.

Forming a Game Plan

Opinions differ on exactly how much one should plot out a game plan in advance of a match. Some golfers prefer to go with the game's ebb and flow, while others feel more confident when prepared for various eventualities.

Whatever your style, some degree of pre-match planning is always wise. Just don't pour all your efforts into strategizing.

"I think too many people get too involved before a match, then they get very nervous," says Jacqui Morgan, a veteran match play competitor with a single-figure handicap.

"Some players play better if they just go with the flow."

Because the status of a match can alter your approach at any time, it can be counter-productive to map out a strategy for every tee shot or hole, because you may get locked into certain shots that aren't right for the moment

Instead, identify the areas on the course where aggression is warranted, and those that may require caution. Stick with the game plan in a close match, but be prepared to adjust on the fly as the score and your opponent's play dictate.

Ultimately, any plan should account for the state of your game, plus your typical strengths and weaknesses. If you've struggled to hit the driver straight during practice or recent rounds, consider hitting fairway woods or hybrids whenever possible. Match play is not the time to change your playing style.

"You must recognize what kind of a golfer you are," Tony agrees. "If you're not a long hitter don't try to be a long hitter."

Game Plan Checklist

Ask and answer these questions to map out your strategy, and then stick with it as much as possible during the match:

- What parts of my game are strong at the moment? Which parts are weak?
- Will I use driver or an iron/fairway wood/hybrid on shorter holes?
- In which situations should I lay up? When should I go for it?
- Will I use putter or wedge if I'm just off the green?
- At what point (ahead or behind) should I become more aggressive or conservative?

- How will I ensure my opponent doesn't get under my skin and influence my play?

Embrace the Elements

You're a golfer, so you don't mind being out in the elements. However, you may be scheduled to play on a day when extreme weather is predicted, so be prepared. Taking the weather into account can also be a very strategic move.

Check the forecast and if rain is expected, take extra towels and gloves. Ensure your wet weather jacket and pants have been re-waterproofed. Consider putting a small collapsible umbrella in your bag to keep you dry on the green while a big golf umbrella protects your bag. Make sure your bag cover keeps the rain out and your club grips dry.

On a hot day be sure to have plenty of icy water, a hat, umbrella, sunscreen etc. It is also important to consider your electrolyte balance if you are a profuse sweater and the humidity is very high. Drink plenty of fluid (at least 1.5 - 2 litres) that has glucose and electrolyte replacements. Eat every couple of hours, preferably snacks such as fruit and nuts. Keep in the shade as much as possible.

But the real key here is the strategy of your mind – most players complain about the rain and it usually puts them off their game. If you approach inclement conditions with the attitude that 'I have a better chance of winning today because I love to play in the rain', you will go in with more confidence and be in a better mental state than your opponent.

Remember that the weather is outside your control, so there is no point in complaining and getting upset – this will simply trigger your brain into a threat state and out of the flow state you need it to be in to play your best golf.

Mental Preparation

Inevitably you'll think about a match beforehand — perhaps days ahead of time, or maybe only hours. The worst that you can do is psyche yourself out by over-analysing or dwelling on negative thoughts.

If you establish an optimistic mindset going in, your results will reflect it. Recognize that every opponent is beatable. Replay past successes in your mind and visualize positive results, such as crushing a perfect opening tee shot or polishing off a 3-metre putt to win a hole.

Prepare to play with a process versus outcome approach, focusing on your pre-shot routine and controlling those elements you <u>can</u> control. The results will take care of themselves.

• *Defeating the 'Gremlin'*

In ***Golf Mind Play: Outsmarting your brain to play your BEST golf*** I discuss the little creature inside us all that embodies negativity — the infamous 'Golf Gremlin'. Unfortunately, this Gremlin is as nasty during match play as it is in stroke play. Then again, the same tactics can be used to defeat him.

> *The Gremlin is responsible for sending negative messages that cause us to berate ourselves and lose confidence in our abilities. The more we give in to the Gremlin, the less we will succeed.*

> *On the golf course, your Gremlin appears when you have already mentally set yourself up for failure. An example is teeing off while there is a crowd of people watching. A common fear shared by many players in this situation is that they will embarrass themselves by slicing the ball or by scuffing it just off the tee. With thoughts like these suffused in your mind, you are actually*

setting yourself up to do exactly what you fear will happen. ...

While dwelling on negative suggestions, players use up precious mental energy that could be more effectively applied to the positive thinking that results in executing a great shot. By listening to your Gremlin, you actually change the chemistry of your brain and create tension in your body.

Golf is a game of flow and feel, and it is almost impossible to hit a good shot when your brain chemistry is causing you to be tense. Blocking out your Gremlin does take practice, but in the long run learning to conquer destructive thinking will make you a more confident player, and allow you to enjoy your game even when you're not playing your best.

The Gremlin can strike in many of the same instances during match play as in stroke play. He may also rear his annoying head when you're facing a formidable opponent — say, a golfer with a big reputation, or someone who has beaten you in the past.

Dealing with the Gremlin means learning to suppress your negative thoughts. Use your mental energy to focus on the present and you'll keep self-doubt at bay. You can do it!

Know the Course

When playing an unfamiliar course, try to get in a practice round or two prior to the match. This is the time to take note of any tricky or deceptive features, such as hidden hazards. Determine if putts tend to break in a general direction — toward a large body of water, for instance.

Also, think about tweaking your club-set make up based on the course's demands. Perhaps a lob wedge would come in handy, or a hybrid with added loft. Check out where flags tend to be placed – every golf course is different.

Make notes based on where you want to place the ball, keeping them all framed in the positive. If you write notes such as 'Beware the hazard on the left', your mind will be drawn to that hazard. Instead, phrase it positively: 'Tee shot best right-hand side of fairway, approach shot aim for back of green', and so forth.

If a practice round isn't possible, use other resources to study up. The Internet provides copious information on many golf courses, including scorecards, hole-by-hole maps and inside tips from the club pro. These can help determine whether the course is long and open or short and tight, and provide clues to what shots may work best. Numerous dogleg right holes may favour a consistent fade, for instance.

You can also search online for reviews by other golfers, or even solicit opinions in a local golf forum. Most players are more than happy to share insights on a course's conditions and idiosyncrasies.

Also keep in mind that match play rules allow you onto the course you are competing on that day. Take advantage of this and have a practice session on greens closest to the clubhouse. If you are nervous starter you may even like to play the first couple of holes if you get there in plenty of time.

In any team competition, always set aside time for a short motivational talk with your mates before your group is called to the tee.

Know Your Foe

If you're facing a familiar opponent, size up their strengths and weaknesses before the match. Are they a big hitter but prone to making mistakes? A steady, down-the-middle type who rarely gives away a hole? A hothead given to emotional outbursts? A good putter? A poor one? A chatterbox?

When the opponent is an unknown quantity, don't waste valuable time scouting their game. Within the first few holes of the match, you'll have a feel for their skills and how they react to different situations.

However they play, don't let it get to you! And never allow your opponent's play to distract you from your own.

Enjoy the Game

This may sound trite, but losing can be more rewarding than winning poorly.

If you have played at a level higher than you normally would, and then left the course believing you played the best you could and that you've learned lessons for next time, what could be better?

Conversely, winning a match where there are disputes over rules and gamesmanship that affect both your and your opponent's performance is not fun - is it?

Golf, after all, is a game — and a game is played for enjoyment and recreation!

Preparation Checklist

When preparing for a match, always take care of the little details in advance. The last thing you want is to be rushing around the morning of the match doing things you could have gotten out of the way beforehand.

Follow this simple checklist to ensure you're relaxed and focused on match day:

2-3 Days Before the Match:
Prepare Your Equipment

- ✓ Clean your clubs and check you have no more than 14 in your bag.
- ✓ Clean your golf shoes and make sure the spikes are in good condition.
- ✓ Put at least one new ball in your bag to start with.

- ✓ Pack a good glove and plenty of tees and markers.
- ✓ Plan your food intake for the round.
- ✓ Have a water bottle ready to go.
- ✓ Pack wet weather gear.
- ✓ If you have an electric buggy, make sure it's fully charged.

The Night Prior: Visualisation

- ✓ Find a quiet place for a few minutes of visualisation — when you first get into bed is always a good time.
- ✓ Picture yourself on the first tee, swinging with ease and flow.
- ✓ Visualise your ball landing on the ideal spot for an approach to the green.
- ✓ The next shot is perfectly executed into the green.
- ✓ You line up your putt, stroke it smoothly and hear it drop into the cup.
- ✓ Continue this for each hole on the course.
- ✓ Feel good about yourself and your game.

Morning of the Match:
Get Your Body Ready

- ✓ Eat a good breakfast — fruit with cereal or an egg on toast - protein is very important.
- ✓ Pack snacks and water into your bag — fruit, nuts etc.
- ✓ Arrive with plenty of time for a warm-up session.
- ✓ Double-check your tee time to make sure no changes have been made.
- ✓ Stretch your muscles, concentrating on the arms, shoulders, back and hamstrings.

The Warm-up

- ✓ Head for the practice nets or driving range and hit 4 - 5 balls with your 7-iron.
- ✓ Hit 4 - 5 balls with your 5-iron, then your 5-wood and lastly a couple with your driver.
- ✓ Now move to the chipping area and chip 10 or so balls.
- ✓ Then onto the putting green for 10 or so putts.

- ✓ Now onto the 9th or 18th green, close to the clubhouse, for 10 minutes of chipping and putting.
- ✓ Now is not the time for swing corrections.
- ✓ Keep your thoughts positive.

Don't Forget to...

- ✓ Set your clothing out the night before.
- ✓ Figure out how long it will take to get to the course, keeping in mind potentially heavy traffic is no excuse for delaying your tee off time and a penalty may occur.
- ✓ Check the Local Rules for the day.
- ✓ Prepare your course notes.
- ✓ Always mark your ball to identify it. Show your opponent on the first tee and ask what they are playing. Very important when they hit into the trees.

Tips

1. Reducing stress by being well-prepared, both physically and mentally, is the key.

2. Rehearse your game in your mind the night before the match.

3. Prepare your equipment and yourself so you are not only looking good but feeling good as well!

III
MATCH PLAY STRATEGY

"A little gamesmanship can go a long way. Just ask your opponent, 'So, do you breathe in or out when you swing?'"
Brad Wuhs, PGA professional

Golf is a game of strategy, especially when the format is match play. As in stroke play, the golfer must determine the best plan for each hole based on its design, the weather and other factors. They must also consider the score of the match as it progresses, their opponent's play and demeanour, their own strengths and weaknesses, and when putts should be conceded.

Here is your guide to managing the strategic elements that make match play so compelling.

Playing the Course v Playing the Opponent

Stroke play, where many competitors vie for the lowest total score, primarily pits the golfer against the course. But what about match play, where head-to-head competition can sharpen the focus on a sole adversary?

While you must pay some attention to your opponent, the bigger focus should remain on the course, your game and your routine. You need to 'get into the zone' and stay there for the duration of the match. No matter how your foe is faring, you must keep a steady mindset if you are to win. The best players find a balance between keeping tabs on the opponent and staying focused. Don't allow an opponent's actions or remarks to affect your performance. Finding that place in the 'zone' will help you overcome any outside influences.

"(My goal) is to play the course," Jacqui Morgan says, "because too many people get tied up playing the opponent. If there is bad play, then you tend to play down to them, rather than playing to your ability."

Always be aware of how many strokes your opponent has taken on the hole, and carefully note any penalties that they may have incurred by hitting into a hazard, an unplayable lie, out of bounds, and so on. Your place in the game at any given moment can affect your approach to the remainder of the hole.

Take a moment to appraise your opponent's skill with short putts to decide if, when and from what length concessions are in order. And assess whether they're mistake-prone or rock-steady as this can help you determine if conservative play will get the job done, or if a bit of risk-taking is necessary.

Otherwise, concentrate on executing the most appropriate shots based on the state of your game and the conditions.

Match Play v Stroke Play Strategy

Match play strategy differs from stroke play in many ways. Since match play requires constant monitoring of your score against a single opponent, your strategies should be regularly altered during the round.

Let's say the match is tied when your opponent hits a fantastic shot to relatively close birdie range. You must decide whether to play aggressively in an attempt to match their anticipated birdie, or to play a safe shot and hope they miss. If you've watched them closely, you can make an educated guess as to their chances of holing the putt.

Here's another hypothetical situation: You're still off the green when your opponent holes out, leaving you no choice but to chip directly for the hole in order to earn a half. Attempting this type of shot in stroke play will add an extra stroke (or more) if you miss, but in match play, an extra stroke is irrelevant – you will either tie or lose the hole.

That's why it's important not only to know your own score at every point on a hole, but your opponent's as well. Always be aware of how many strokes you are leading or trailing by, and adjust your strategy accordingly. Having said that, it is also important not to be too focused on their score – that is completely outside your circle of control (*see* **Golf Mind Play: Outsmarting your brain to play your BEST golf** for tips on how to deal with this).

It is a good habit to check number of shots with each other when you reach every green. Ask your opponent how many strokes they are to the green before you begin putting – that way it's easier to double check if there is a discrepancy. Always assume your opponent will sink every putt, so there are no surprises!

Playing Aggressively v Playing Conservatively

Golfers may play conservatively in certain circumstances, such as when they're leading a match, or when their opponent has found trouble on a hole, or when the opponent has an especially difficult shot he is unlikely to execute.

Paradoxically, conservative play carries an element of risk. For instance, a trailing foe may attempt 'hero shots' to reclaim the lead. If they pull off a couple of miraculous recoveries, your conservative approach may backfire by leaving you no chance of matching their birdie or par. Don't be disheartened – keep playing steadily and it's likely you can make a comeback.

Aggressiveness is more acceptable in match play because risks are lower than in stroke play. After all, a botched shot costs no more than the loss of a single hole, as opposed to the big number (double bogey or worse) that can wreck a scorecard in stroke play. This can happen to the best of us – pros and amateurs alike.

That's not to suggest you should always opt for the aggressive approach — there's a time and place for it. If you're leading near round's end, maintaining maximum focus on the middle of fairways and greens, rather than cutting off doglegs or aiming straight at flagsticks, will prevent costly mistakes.

You must also assess your chances of success on a risky shot, regardless of the score.

"The overriding factor," Tony McAllister says, "is that you can do it. If you can't do it, don't do it."

If there is any doubt in your mind, then your body will not perform at its best. Go with your gut instinct and trust it.

Hero Shots – When to Go for It

As the match play format offers relatively low risk for bold play, there are times when going for a so-called 'hero shot' is often the best option, when the odds are stacked against you.

Example: In a tied match, your opponent has found the green in two on a par 4, with par a near-certainty and birdie a distinct possibility. Meanwhile, your ball sits in the rough, with a tree blocking the path to the green. In stroke play, the wise golfer would pitch sideways into the fairway to limit the damage. In match play, you may as well try and knock the ball over the tree to give yourself an outside shot of saving a half, or squaring the hole.

That way, match play alleviates the pressure of decision-making and gives the golfer a shot at being, yes, a hero.

"The hero shot is all about drama and performance," Tony says. "The hero shot is showing off all that you can do out there on the golf course. I love playing the hero shot probably twice in a match. You'll know when it's needed."

Indeed, if you believe you can salvage a half (or even win the hole) without heroics, then safe play is best. This is where you need to consider the low risk - high percentage shot.

Conceding as a Strategy

Conceding putts is an integral part of match play strategy. In general, putts of 15cm or less are conceded as a common courtesy, although putts at the outer limit of that range are open for consideration.

Assess your opponent's putting skills to determine which putts to concede. If he is having a bad day on the greens, don't concede short putts that you believe he might miss.

One concession tactic is for you to offer generous 'gimmes' early in the game, then refrain later so as to apply the pressure on your opponent. Players are more likely to miss a 30cm putt if they haven't attempted any during the round, while making a short putt or two on the outward holes gives a player confidence for those tension-filled 'knee-knockers' on the back nine.

Keep in mind that your opponent cannot ask to be given this kind of shot – although they may well try it on you!

Never concede on side-slope putts or downhill putts – they already have a tendency to raise the tension in your opponent's hands, often leading to a mis-stroke and a missed putt!

"When the heat is on, you need to recognize that now is the time to call upon your opponent to make that shot," Tony advises.

The Other Side of Concessions

Indeed, concessions can be tricky business. As a general rule, never expect a concession from an opponent, no matter how routine a putt you face.

Being prepared to hole out on every green is key to maintaining steady nerves when called upon.

Sometimes an opponent will concede a relatively lengthy putt – say one metre – with the unspoken expectation that you'll return the favour later on. You're under no obligation to do so — in fact, this may well be a sign of your foe's discomfort over short putts.

Always state out loud that you are giving them the putt, if that is what you decide to do, and before they pick up say "so that would be in for 5?"

This confirms the number of strokes they've taken so there is no confusion. Keep in mind that once the ball is picked up, that putt cannot be replayed and that a 'gimme' actually counts as one stroke!

Be polite, but don't let an opponent's apparent generosity influence your decisions.

Opening Tee Shot is Key

Strategies tend to come into focus as players are well entrenched in the match, but executing your game plan at the first tee can make the difference between leading the entire round and struggling to keep up.

Let's say you have the honour. This is when a solid shot off the first tee can apply a great deal of pressure on your opponent, dictating strategy for the match. On the other hand, an opening slice or hook gives your competitor an advantage by completely relieving the pressure. Assuming they find the fairway, your opponent now has the option of a conservative or aggressive approach, and an opportunity to seize control from the start.

Remember – your opponent is just as nervous as you are. Now is the time to focus on the present and let go of any thoughts around the outcome for the day. Simply pick a target on the fairway and aim for that. Take a few deep breaths and focus.

Then all you have to do is maintain this strategy on every other tee.

Pre-Shot Routine

The pre-shot routine is very important no matter your level of play. If you watch the pros, note how they typically perform the identical routine before each shot.

Your pre-shot routine sets the stage to make your best swing. Consistency is the key. When you have a simple visualisation strategy to centre and focus your mind on, you will play far better golf. Keep it simple, include an alignment reference, a relaxed practice swing, alignment of the clubface and a look at the target, then make your swing.

Once you have made a shot selection, and this may be conservative or 'go for it' then it's time to execute the shot. Step up to the ball with confidence that you will be making the shot exactly as planned. Any doubt in your mind will transfer to your body and you will play a poor shot

Your pre-shot routine will help you to set up, calm and prepare your golf muscles and ultimately improve your chances of success.

Tips

1. While you must pay some attention to your opponent, the bigger focus should remain on the course, your game and your routine.

2. Don't always opt for the aggressive approach – there's a time and place for it. First determine the risk to reward ratio.

3. Never concede short downhill or side lying putts – it will put pressure on your opponent to sink what they know is a more difficult putt!

IV

THE MIND IN MATCH PLAY

*"If you try to fight the course,
it will beat you."*

Lou Graham, 1975 US Open champion

Match play demands balance. Balanced thinking, balanced attitude, balanced emotions (both inward and external). While mercurial players will win their share, the even-keeled golfer will fare better over the long haul.

This chapter will help you deal with the game's inevitable ups and downs.

It's All About Balance

Of course, match play is full of sudden momentum shifts and unexpected turnabouts, so maintaining balance is easier said than done. Match play requires you to get your head into the right zone before hitting the course. If you're well prepared emotionally, then you are streaks ahead already.

Think positively, don't get down on yourself and above all, go out there to enjoy the match.

Make sure you're dressed comfortably and you're presenting yourself well. This will automatically give you an edge. On the flip side, your opponent will automatically feel they have one over you if you turn up in crumpled clothes with odd socks!

Dealing with Adversity

It is crucial to analyse your opponent's strengths and weaknesses as soon as possible so you can identify openings in their game and take an early advantage. It's important to remember that your opponent is watching you too, which is why it's better to show your poker face when under stress, rather than getting angry or throwing a club when you miss a shot.

Revealing negative emotions in match play signals to your opponent that you're struggling and that you may be more receptive to negative suggestions (see the section on Gamesmanship later in this chapter). Displaying your weak side can also raise their confidence, and provide them with an opportunity to step on you when you're down.

Conversely, when your opponent loses control of their emotions, you can be sure that if their mindset doesn't change quickly, they'll be easy to beat. Playing conservatively from this point forward might be all it takes to maintain the lead or forge ahead, because their frustration alone will wreak havoc on their game.

Falling behind your opponent is enough to shake the nerves, disrupt your concentration and allow your gremlin to rear his ugly head. Match play success often hinges on your ability to avoid this trap, and put your gremlin back in his box!

Golf Mind Play: Outsmarting your brain to play your BEST golf tells us how:

> *By listening to your Gremlin, you actually change the chemistry of your brain and create tension in your body. Golf is a game of flow and feel, and it is almost impossible to hit a good shot when your brain chemistry is causing you to be tense.*
>
> *If you submit to negative thoughts, they become extremely difficult to overcome. The key is to gain control of your thinking by replacing pessimism with optimism and by substituting negative suggestions with phrases that resemble "I can do this" or "I can swing with the perfect*

tempo". You can recite these thoughts just as easily as the evil Gremlin can sow new negative ones.

By conjuring up a positive attitude where you would normally have a negative impulse, you'll wipe the slate clean and allow yourself a fair chance of hitting a good ball, and feel good about yourself at the end of your game.

This format rewards assertiveness; so if you're behind, don't let anxiety surrounding a much-needed hero shot prevent you from trying it. Always remember, the worst that can happen is the loss of a single hole. If you're lagging behind and frustrated, then building up your confidence and motivation will bring your hero shot to fruition. You can feed off the stress of pressure for energy and inspiration. Always look for a way to turn a situation to your advantage, and never let your opponent dictate the outcome of a shot.

Never panic if you're trailing early in the game. Exercise patience and look for an opening where you can turn the tables. Remember, the outcome depends on how you score in relation to your competitor, so you can play the worst game of your life and still win.

Jacqui Morgan offers some sound advice for dealing with pressure-packed moments and those times when a match seems to be slipping away.

"When something goes bad, go back to basics," she says. "Think of the swing's rhythm" and just go back to the tempo of the lapping wave.

You can learn more about how to get your rhythm back and how to create the image of the wave in *Golf Mind Play: Outsmarting your brain to play your BEST golf*

Dealing with Success

When you gain a big lead, you must protect yourself against overconfidence, complacency or worse, feeling sorry for your opponent – it's lethal in match play. If you play too cautiously or become brash, your foe will detect the change and try to use it to their advantage. The elation of being ahead may shift your focus away from your game, then before you know it, your opponent will be right on your tail and you're faced with real pressure.

Stick with your regular routine. Keep in mind that your opponent can hit a match altering shot at any time. In fact, no matter how poorly they may be playing, always expect them to turn things around on the very next shot, otherwise you risk letting your guard down and letting them back into the match with your own sloppy play.

Just like dealing with adversity, dealing with success requires a steady, even-keeled approach. Complacency is just as dangerous as frustration or negative emotion.

The Element of Surprise

Match play is a game of momentum, where one great shot can reverse the fortunes of an apparently beaten foe. That's why you should always expect the unexpected, and always anticipate that your foe will play their best shot each and every time.

Example: You've landed your tee shot nicely in the middle of the fairway while your opponent has a difficult shot from thick rough. The odds are clearly in your favour. Then your foe blasts a career-best shot onto the green, within a few metres of the hole. If you had mentally chalked up a win before their shot, you'll now have to recover from the surprise in order to execute a similar shot. If, however, you remain present in the moment — focused on your task and expecting such a result from your opponent — nothing will have changed and you can now hit your shot onto the green, too, as planned.

It's doubly vital to expect the best from your opponent on the greens. Remember, they can hole out from anywhere, while a three-putt is always a possibility on your part. Just because you're closer to the cup don't assume the hole is won. It is not over until that ball is in the hole!

Gamesmanship

Unfortunately, match play brings out the worst in some golfers, whose competitive instincts trump sportsmanship. These players may use tactics, often subtle, designed to distract you or plant the seeds of negative thought in your mind.

Dealing with this kind of gamesmanship proves difficult for some, but it needn't be. If you have a clear idea of what gamesmanship is all about, then you are already in front, because you will be alert to what your opponent is up to if they try to bring it on!

A player does not have to use gamesmanship to win, but an education in this area prevents the opponent from getting the upper hand. Embrace gamesmanship, as it is what match play is all about. Sure, none of us enjoy, nor should we put up with nasty tactics, but all of use some form of it — from playing quickly or slowly, being chatty, not conceding putts and so on.

The best ploy to use is attitude and outward confidence, even if you are shaking like a leaf inside. If that first tee shot is hit with purpose down the middle, your opponent is already thinking, 'This guy is good!' If your opponent believes he or she can't win, they won't!

Don't allow your opponent to bully you or convince you to agree with their requests. Know the rules, and always refer to the rules book or referee, if there is one. If you are unsure, ask your opponent to show you where the rules cover their request.

Here's how I've personally handled an instance of gamesmanship:

When playing an interclub match play competition, my opponent was quite talkative to begin with and wanted to engage in a lot of idle chit-chat. She would walk beside me and talk right up to my ball, offering comments like "That's a difficult lie — might be tough to get out of!" or, as we were walking onto the next tee, saying, "Last time I played this hole I went into that hazard on the left twice off the tee" – just as I was about to hit. To deal with this, I just smiled, took a deep breath, practised 'being present in the moment' by listening to the sounds of nature around me, which blocked her chatter out. I took an extra moment to re-group, focused on my target and ended up hitting my shot of the day!

There can also be the paper rattler, the bag zipper, the gossiper, the nice-as-pie, the self-admonisher, the grumpy aggressor, the jacket-velcro-ripper, the glove velcro ripper – these are all the opponents that you may find yourself up against. But don't fear! If paired with any one of these personalities, simply separate yourself physically from them as you leave the tee. Once you've hit, get ready to walk off straight away, and walk ahead so they are not at your side. If they persist then politely mention that you prefer a little quiet time before hitting — they should get the message.

It's best to give yourself a minute or two of silent switch-on time before each shot to consider your lie, the wind, the preferred landing spot, club selection etc. The last thing you need is a competitor undermining your concentration.

Tips

1. When in doubt, play conservatively. Look for the low-risk, high-percentage shot. If you attempt to play to your handicap, chances are you will beat your opponent 90% of the time.

2. Staying present and not letting your mind dwell on past bad shots will keep your

adrenaline down and your body calm. Try listening to the surrounding natural sounds to get into a present state. What birds can you hear? What other sounds? Allow them to keep you 'present'.

3. Be aware of your partner's gamesmanship – do not try to outdo it! Be your natural self and ignore their attempts at unnerving you.

V

MAXIMISE YOUR OPPORTUNITIES

"Hit the shot you know you can hit, not the one you think you should."

Dr Bob Rotella, premier sport psychologist

What's the most important part of the game in match play? How you play the course? Putting? Driving? Chipping and pitch shots?

This depends on the course, the conditions and how your opponent is playing. However, there are certain skills that will serve you well regardless of the variables — the ability to hole short putts, for example, or consistently finding the fairway.

Develop the specific skills detailed here and you'll become a match play ace.

Course Management

Course management comes into play on every shot, with some shots being more important than others. Managing your mind is a key match play component. So is managing the golf course.

Efficient course management is your ability to play the golf course the way it was designed, avoiding trouble and placing the ball in the best position to hit the next shot. It requires you to plan and concentrate before every hit.

The game of golf is about managing imperfections. The golf course is set up so you will make hundreds of decisions over the few hours that you play. Course management is about playing smart golf and thinking positively to avoid mistakes. Golf is about managing yourself around the course without letting your ego take over.

When you change the way your mind sees the golf course, you will see opportunities, rather than problems. You'll see where you want to hit the ball, not the hazards or trouble areas that should be avoided.

Not every golfer understands the nuances involved in plotting a proper path from tee to green. Those who do often gain a big advantage. What's more, course management is one element over which you can have near-total control. While nobody makes perfect decisions every time, being absolutely clear on a few central tenets greatly improves your percentages. It is important to have a strategy for playing each hole so you will be prepared ahead of time to handle the feelings that might arise to distract you.

Since match play strategy is partly determined by your opponent's play and partly determined by the score, no rule is set in stone. In any match, you're likely to adjust your course management approach based on the situation at the time.

Nonetheless, your personal course management style — just like your swing — should be consistent from hole to hole and also game to game.

For starters, your on-course mentality should fit your personality. If you're a pedal-to-the-metal Type-A guy or gal, you'll play best in that mode, while more cautious types will do better when avoiding big risks.

Regardless of your style, one rule generally applies to course management in a match between players of similar handicaps: **Don't give away holes**. In the famous words "It ain't over until the fat lady sings!" or more correctly for match play golfers "It ain't over until the ball is in the hole!"

At the amateur level, the most certain route to victory is to position yourself to win or half every hole. While that may run counter to the idea that match play's low risk levels invite aggressive play, it underscores the need to carefully pick spots for going out strongly.

Course Management Checklist

To develop an effective, consistent course management approach you need to keep these things in mind:

- ✓ Knowing the layout of the holes before you play will give you a sense of confidence – check those notes you made during your practice round or cast an eye over your download of the course layout. It really does help.

- ✓ Aim to hit the green in regulation for **your** game and not what a scratch marker would hit. This will relieve the pressure and set you up for an easy par for your handicap.

- ✓ Play your **own game** and play the shot that will make your next hit as easy as possible. For instance, if you are in trouble in some trees, rather than whack it straight through them, this is the time to play cautiously, so use the next shot to get yourself into a position where you have a clear go at the following hit.

- ✓ Playing to the centre of greens relieves pressure on your irons, short game and putting.

- ✓ Be aware of flag placement. It's easy to lose shots by misreading the location of the hole.

- ✓ Many greens slope from back to front, so if this is the case, play short of the flag when hitting to a rear pin placement. Going long often leaves a difficult chip or pitch.

- ✓ Don't let an opponent's playing style affect yours. If they're a longer hitter than you, so be it. Trying to keep up is a recipe for disaster. Play your **own game**.

- ✓ Don't force shots that you're not comfortable hitting. If your natural ball flight is left-to-right, avoid attempting draws. You're better off playing your usual fade, even if it means hitting away from the flag — there will be plenty of holes where your customary shot will prove advantageous.

- ✓ You'll often hit the ball farther when your adrenaline is flowing freely – at the end of a tight match, for instance. Steady down! Dial back your club selection when you're pumped up (e.g. hit 9-iron instead of an 8) and stay very focused on the present.

Driving

Long drivers are known to intimidate match play opponents, especially at the amateur level. Accurate driving, though, can prove frustrating to watch, much like a competitor with a hot putter.

Whether you fall into the category of 'bomber' or 'steady Eddie', your competitive advantage can become a mental edge.

Big hitters

If you reliably hit big and long, flex your muscle when opportunity knocks. For example, when playing a drivable par 4, or a par 5 that's within your reach in two, go for it! Match play offers less risk than stroke play, so don't fear making that aggressive shot when facing a foe who lacks your power.

Straight hitters

Play to your strength. Focus on getting every tee shot on the fairway, even if it means eschewing the driver on occasion. Playing long from the short grass takes pressure off your approach game, forcing your opponent to post a mistake-free round.

Irons & Approach Play

Getting those iron shots close to the pin is always a plus, but it shouldn't be your primary objective. Giving yourself a chance to win or half every hole is ideal.

Your goal should be to hit as many greens in regulation (for your handicap) as possible. More often than not, that means simply aiming for the centre of the green and steering clear of trouble spots like bunkers, water or the 'short side' of a green (where there's little room between your ball and the flag).

Fact is — a ball in the middle of a green is usually within 10 metres of the cup and often less than 7 metres away. Playing for the centre not only helps you avoid off-green trouble, it also cuts down your three-putt percentage – alleviating much of the pressure that comes with match play.

There's a time to be more aggressive with your irons, of course. Any shot with a wedge is an opportunity to attack. Likewise, when the pin is in a safe position, with no forced carries over hazards, a bold play may be in order.

Chipping, Pitching & Bunkers

A sound short game is another crucial element to match play success. Again, watching a foe extricate themselves from trouble to save halves – or even win holes – can grind down a player's resolve.

The ability to get up-and-down (chip on and then sink the putt in one) is a tremendous asset for your own psyche. The positive effects of good chipping, pitching and bunker play can spread to other parts of your game and before you know it, you're driving the ball up the fairway and hitting greens with regularity which, ironically, negates the need for short-game wizardry.

While miraculous saves can prove pivotal in match play, it's most important to make the routine up-and-down. In practice, work primarily on straightforward chips, pitches and bunker shots, setting aside a few minutes at the end to try more challenging fare.

Putting

Matches between equals often come down to who putts best on the day. Putting also plays a huge role in the psychological battle.

If you carry putting confidence into a match, you're essentially 1-up before the first shot is struck. Nothing wears down an opponent more than a series of hole-outs. Conversely, a few missed putts can deflate your own competitive sails and bolster your foe's.

The process of concessions makes putting all the more important. As mentioned previously, you should never expect an opponent to concede a putt, no matter how short. But hole a few knee-knockers and your opponent will know they can't rely on you missing a tap-in and handing them a win.

Schedule at least a couple of practice putting sessions during the week prior to a match. Focus on putts under 2 metres to shore up this part of your game. It will pay off on match day.

Tips

1. Ensure you get a practice round on the course you are competing on the week or two before your match. Take notes that reflect where you want the ball to land on most shots – not listing hazards or places you don't want your ball to go.

2. If your opponent is longer off the tee than you, or a better chipper or putter, then congratulate them in your mind and always expect that type of shot from them. That way your confidence won't be shattered when they pull off the spectacular shots.

3. Project an air of confidence about you, even if you may be feeling a little nervous! The old adage 'fake it 'til you make it' works well in match play.

Appendix

Game Plan Checklist

Ask and answer these questions to map out your strategy, and then stick with it as much as possible during the match:

- ☐ Which parts of my game are strong at the moment? Which parts are weak?

    - Driving
        Strong/Weak/Average
    - Fairway woods & hybrids
        Strong/Weak/Average
    - Middle and long irons
        Strong/Weak/Average
    - Short irons
        Strong/Weak/Average
    - Chipping & pitching
        Strong/Weak/Average
    - Bunker play
        Strong/Weak/Average
    - Short putting (within 1m)
        Strong/Weak/Average
    - Mid-range putting (1-10m)
        Strong/Weak/Average

- Long putting (beyond 10m)
  Strong/Weak/Average

☐ Will I use a driver or an iron/fairway wood/hybrid on shorter holes?

☐ In which situations should I lay up? When should I go for it?

☐ Will I use a putter or a wedge if I'm just off the green?

☐ At what point (ahead or behind) should I become more aggressive or conservative?

☐ How will I ensure the opponent doesn't get under my skin and influence my decisions with gamesmanship or their style of play?

Preparation Checklist

When preparing for a match, always take care of the little details in advance. The last thing you want is to rush around on the morning of the match doing things you could have sorted out beforehand.

Follow this simple checklist to put you in a relaxed, focused mindset when it's time to play:

2-3 Days Before the Match: Prepare Your Equipment

- ☐ Clean your clubs and check you have no more than 14 in your bag.

- ☐ Clean your golf shoes and make sure the spikes are in good condition.

- ☐ Put at least one new ball in your bag to begin play and make sure it's marked.

- ☐ Pack a fresh glove and plenty of tees and markers.

- ☐ Plan your food intake for the round.

- ☐ Have a water bottle ready to go.

- ☐ Pack wet weather gear at all times even if rain's is not predicted.

- ☐ If you have an electric buggy, make sure it's fully charged.

- ☐ Check whether GPS devices are permitted on the course and ensure you have the correct course map downloaded.

- ☐ Make sure you have your rules book with you.

- ☐ Have a pencil and rubber for scoring or making notes regarding disputes.

- ☐ Go over the rules of match play.

The Night Prior: Visualisation

- ☐ Find a quiet place for a few minutes of visualisation — when you first get into bed is always a good time.
- ☐ Picture yourself on the first tee, swinging with ease and flow.
- ☐ Visualise your opening tee shot landing on the ideal spot for the approach.
- ☐ The next shot is perfectly executed into the green.
- ☐ You line up your putt, stroke it smoothly and hear it drop into the cup.
- ☐ Continue this for all the holes on the course.
- ☐ Feel good about yourself and your game.

Morning of the Match: Get Your Body Ready

- ☐ Eat a good breakfast — fruit with cereal or an egg on toast.
- ☐ Pack water and snacks into your bag — fruit, nuts, etc.
- ☐ Arrive with plenty of time for a warm-up session.

- ☐ Double-check your tee time to make sure no changes have been made.
- ☐ Stretch your muscles, concentrating on the arms, shoulders, back and hamstrings.

Warming Up

- ☐ Head for the practice nets or range and hit 4 - 5 balls with your 7-iron.
- ☐ Hit 4 - 5 balls with your 5-iron, then your 5-wood and lastly a couple with your driver.
- ☐ Now move to the chipping area and chip 10 or so balls.
- ☐ Then onto the putting green for 10 or so putts.
- ☐ Go to the ninth or 18th greens and have a few practice chips and putts. Ensure the Golf Club allows you onto the course to practice - it is a rule of golf, however, some Clubs choose to not allow it.
- ☐ Now is **not** the time for swing corrections.
- ☐ Keep your thoughts positive.

Don't Forget to...

- ☐ Set your clothing out the night before.

- ☐ Note phone numbers of club captain, other team members and pro-shop.

- ☐ Figure out how long it will take to get to the course, keeping in mind potentially heavy traffic. Heavy traffic or getting lost are not valid reasons for waiving the potential penalty of disqualification.

- ☐ Check the Local Rules for the day. If relevant to the day's play, check the course's definition of a preferred lie.

- ☐ Prepare your course notes.

- ☐ If you're part of a Pennant team, make sure you're at the course on time for the team briefing.

- ☐ Check where you'll need to go to give your results.

☐

References and Recommended Reading

Carson, Rick, *Taming Your Gremlin: A surprisingly simple method for getting out of your own way*. New York, Harper Collins, 2003

Mack, Gary & Casstevens, David, *Mind Gym: An athlete's guide to inner excellence*, Chicago, McGraw Hill, 2001

Gallwey, W. Timothy, *The Inner Game of Golf*, New York, Random House, 1981

Rotella, Dr Robert, *Golf is not a Game of Perfect*, London, Simon & Schuster, 1995

Parent, Dr Joseph, *Zen Golf: Mastering the mental game*, New York, Random House, 2005

Penick, Harvey, *The Wisdom of Harvey Penick, Collected writings*, New York, Simon & Schuster, 1997

Penick, Harvey, *For all who love the game*, New York, Simon & Schuster, 1995

Reynolds, *Marcia, Outsmart your brain: How to make success feel easy*, Phoenix, Covisioning, 2004

Saunders, Vivien, *The Golfing Mind*, New York, Three Rivers Press, 1995

Tresidder, Tracy, *Golf Mind Play; Outsmarting your brain to play your best golf*, Lightning Source Australia, 2007

To receive your free MP3 of this book, email
tracy@golfmindplay.com
with "Free Match Play MP3" in the subject line.

For personal golf mind coaching, please contact
Tracy Tresidder
tracy@golfmindplay.com
www.golfmindplay.com
Office: +61 2 9924 7078
Mobile: +61 415 980 4176

www.ingramcontent.com/pod-product-compliance
Lightning Source LLC
Chambersburg PA
CBHW071019040426
42443CB00007B/848